PROGRESSION

PROGRESSION

Urban Centigrade®
751 East 161 Street, Apt. 7A
Bronx, NY 10456
www.urbancentigrade.com
Email: wamuhu.mwaura@urbancentigrade.com

Urban Centigrade® logo is proprietary and copyright protected.
Designed by Antony Kamau.

Cover image provided regionally for commercial purposes by Fotolia.
Purchased with full rights and used by permission.
Copyright © creative4m – Fotolia
Lettering and interior design by Wamuhu Mwaura.
Author photograph provided by Joe Allen, Jr.

Ordering Information, quantity sales:

Special discounts are available on quantity purchases by individuals, small businesses, and localized retailers. For details, contact the publisher at the address above. Orders by U.S. trade bookstores and wholesalers, please contact publisher via e-mail above.

ISBN: 978-0-9903043-1-9

Printed in the United States of America

PROGRESSION

SECOND EDITION

JOE ALLEN, JR.

Edited by Wamuhu Mwaura

URBAN
centigrade
Urban Centigrade®
New York

Editor's Note:

Dear Reader,

The first edition of *PROGRESSION* was published in June of 2012 with limited distribution. Now, under the trademark Urban Centigrade® (registered less than a year ago), I find myself honored again by Joe Allen, Jr. in assisting with the re-printing of his body of work.

Editing is never an easy task.

An unforeseen writer, Joe 'Joetry' Allen Jr.'s voice is strong however, his self-reflections honest, captivating, and his method lyrically effective.

With *PROGRESSION*, maintaining a balance between the weight of his words and his very unique voice proved effortless, both times around.

This second edition contains new pieces which seek to strengthen the reader's understanding of the true nature, the progression, of Joe's mental, spiritual and physical journey through the hardships of his life.

Sincerely,
Wamuhu Mwaura
CEO and Editor-in-Chief, Urban Centigrade®

PROGRESSION

In life, change is a part of moving forward. This compilation is a poetically written story of my life. It's relayed to you in a way that may parallel your own lives in some instances and may cause insight in others. The fact that you are now reading this means that you have become an intricate part of my growth, and for that I thank you!

Open your mind and let me open your heart!

<JOETRY>

OTHER WORKS BY URBAN CENTIGRADE

DUES FOR THE REPOSE, FROM WORDS MUCH LIKE POETRY
        WAMUHU MWAURA

TABLE OF CONTENTS

<u>Biological Verse 101</u>

Unfertilized paper be the egg
semen, the confabulation of my choice
explode in orgasmic creation
conceive the minute you combine
not with finished articles or determiners
instead, I interject a conjunction
before a metaphor takes shape and
I am the vertical space between allusion and alliteration
no circular file termination
for any fabrication

– I let breathe –

even if displeased
my existence demands attention
from someone, anyone
this new birth

it's a POEM!

Mother's Day

The presence of your spirit
caused growth
lessons learned
during your absence;
like chocolate to a sweet-tooth
satisfied my wants, and to an extent
babysat my needs
you made sure when hungry
they were fed.

Mother
the eyeglasses of my life
which helped sight the invisible;
my censor
you taught me to listen
to smell out a rat
tuned my senses
as well as my sense
you were my palette
the first taste of success;
through your touch
I touched others
your life's work
made mine livable.

Your title has been well earned
Mother.

Life's Ride

CLICK

What have I done?
Sat down
in fear of losing my breath.

CLICK

Locked in for just
few seconds, scenery screaming
past my screams.

CLICK

All motion stops
as my hair blends
with clouds,

treetops tickle
my sneaker bottoms
anticipating the
loss of my stomach.

WHOOSH

Facial g-force
keeps a smile fastened
to a head whose eyes

3

goose out as being choked –

WHOOSH

– the weightlessness of my situation
has reached in between my legs
and snatched crotch upward.

WHOOSH

Wind like a boxer
pounds my face
with quick jabs, first my left ear
then my right listens closest to the ground.

WHOOSH

Darkness with a twist
light, just as fleet as
the dark.

WHOOSH

Although stationary on my neck,
head spins unbelievably fast
and still I ask,
can I do it again?

My Thoughtless Matter

sits here thinking of nothing,
brain shutting down,
mind contemplating the empty space
it tries desperately to write.

My soul,
like a vacuum,
no available air,
suffocates in lost thought,
feel like I just got snuffed out
by cyclones too hard for cowboys to wrangle.

I ascend stairs of steep incline,
searching for new heights,
perplexed
when I reach one landing to find
more flights
I still have to climb.

When the process
really slows down,
sometimes completely stalls,
I am a still, stone statue in mid-room
surrounded by four walls.

De-Wall Flowered

I arrived

looked for immediate acceptance
took my cue and schlepped into my comfort zone
plastic receptacle in a hand-held tight
back erect, the limit became my box spring
averted eyes searched wisely
refusing to rest on rejection
that fear kept me adhered
to my vertical mattress
admission to my boudoir
never given
trespassers caused me to become
miniscule or practiced
my new disappearing act

peripheral

caught movement approaching
the river flowed from brow to groin
from groin to foot
inertia entered and incited
a block of ice to surround me
to enclose me in shock
asked to exit my imaginary
entrance to my fictitious room
I glided on my
permafrost shoes

melted into fluidity
the motion a sick feeling
wanted to always be there

where the specks of brightness

zip backwards and forwards
up and down
what I detected audibly
in the background
that dictated such animated
moves of ritualistic mating
had ceased
but now as I recessed into
the untrue chambers I created
something had changed
back no longer touched
where I lazed
anxiety set in

although unmoved

I was now the seeker
a new entity to inquire
shall we dance?

Hip Hop

Friends and heads from the neighborhood
Roadie for position
"STEP OUTSIDE THE ROPES PLEASE"
Fame, your five minutes
Being down, part of the setup
Speaker, you, turntables, mixer
Amp, you, fan,
Crates, you, speaker
Can't stay still, huh?

Blending of songs from
Genres unheard
Cohesiveness tight
Fluctuation of hands
By the real musician
Hey D.J., wanna play that song
Keep me dancin' all night
Unregistered movements
Controlled by
Mechanisms powered by
The hanging of extension cords

Five floors deep
Con-Ed cheap
Lamp-post generator
Of the schoolyard sway
Let's dance
Let's dance to the drummer's beat

Do the hustle
Electric boogie shocking
Break dancers' layman for B-Boys
Twirl body, motion blurs vision

Freeze, position lock

Crowd roars
Take a bow
Showmanship on a concrete stage
The cultured playground of song and dance.

Surprising Departure

I see the lights flashing
annoying rays here now gone
from my vantage point
another neighborhood spat
going wrong
the mob gathers up the block
while I drink heavily on the bench
ladies surround me
I am the dollar man tonight.

In my town cars screech
as though in pain
and sounds like fireworks
are ear common
raised voices echo
in cheerfulness
as well as anger
comfortable but unsafe
this is my burg.

As the crowd disperses
normality returns;
curiosity
I ask a passerby
of the happening;
I am assaulted by the reply
beer bottle explodes out of my hand
even 50 yards in one step seems eternal

at once, I see the prone
lunacy by identification
rage by flashing rays
misunderstanding
that chalk lines and blankets
mean closure
to a life so close it's mine.

In reality, it was changed forever
minus one friend
crying!

R.I.P. G-MAN

Stabbed

I literally died once
a few minutes chest pumped
and balloon blown; shocking?
Nah, none of that
still standing.

I trace torso scars
to my neglected past
a sternum piercing
held me back and pushed me forward
simultaneously
beginning my end or
ending my beginning
jump-started my life
until irresponsibly, I let
juices from the boost die
never re-tuning parts
so deterioration was inevitable,

wondering why my engine almost
re-expired while conscious
bogus maintenance
bandaging instead of stitching.
Well, I'm in the shop now
monitoring the job being done
replacing parts of my life
once passed over, but now regained
foot firmly on the pedal

diagnostically content
breaking with caution

AWARE, AWAKE, ALIVE!

Fear

I held hands and waltzed with the waves apprehensively
preconceived notions of octopi and sea monsters

like driftwood floating through my brain
with my human periscope up

I realized the importance of the inhale, exhale theory
for with my periscope down, any act of breathing

could bring impending doom;
upper and lower extremities trembled

with the undetermined way of the current
courage built to a crescendo

then nodded like a corner dope fiend
this trial of choice, to fight or run

like treading water;
my soaking wet thoughts dripped with recollection

of a man who said he feared nothing
hearing of his exploits and untimely death

for bringing a stick to a gunfight
helped me resuscitate my resources

now determined body movements

propelled me to survive

reaching for the edge of life's pool
I pulled myself up and here I stand

the dreadful feeling overcome
fear.

Still Peeking

Playing catch up
Confused
Physically I muse
Mentally I run
Forward facing
Backward tracing
Looking for missing chapters
Within text of stone
Unalterable

Jogging memory
Rearward in motion
Backtracking for expectations
Still unreached
Knowing the re-starting line
Means optimism
As racers look ahead

Pre-sighting goals
Causes continuous thinking
Patterns
Like shifting gears
Grinding within change
I downshift
To see the humongous imagery
The big picture (sidebar)
Realizing this race
Even if in first place

JOE ALLEN, JR.

Is never won

Even with the right direction
Its length eternal
Mile by Mile by Mile
You never catch up!

Me Who? #1

As I look into the unfolding mirror
Of valuable elapsed time
A twisted story appears before me
That has no reason, no rhyme
An historical jumbling of events
Giving hints about my past
Just an inkling of my being.

Who am I? I still must ask;
How dare you judge me?
Deem me uncouth, with such miniscule, a peek
Call me names or give me praise
Because I have yet to speak
Using my oral cavity
Which vocalizes thought
Gives you the description of a package
That's frequently store bought
But when secluded quietly in a corner
Where the light just faintly glows
There is this ever learning and changing character
The me that no one knows.

Me Who? #2

I am made of
Each flake of an inconsistent snowstorm
Continuously appearing
One after another
Form ever changing
Like moods, no two alike.

Accumulation of said forms
Adheres structurally;
Lego blocks of white
Interlocking substance
Built into a mass growth
Molded through time.

Breaks of the downfallen
Re-shape intricate patterns
The editor of erosion, Nature
Removes what's unwanted
Causing the flowing away of
Soon to be sewage.

Remainder piled upon once more
Patent number the same
As modification and acclimatization
Of future storms
I may face,

Constant yet yielding

PROGRESSION

The same but altered
Stands The Me No One Knows
Because as my last word
Of verse is spoken, a new storm is brewing
And evidence of change is apparent.

Self-Service Station

Hey you, yeah you,
there's something about you I don't like.

You walk as though
the moment your sole touches down

an instant melody
of welcoming tunes

plays out loud
when all the while the morbid rhythm

of your inner soul
rips the harmony

out of all you stand for
the smile on your face

a mask
a false ray of sunshine

a frown,
the tornado

of un-felt emotions
deadened by formula

who are you?

PROGRESSION

If I had my guess,

not the person you want to be
changes are in store

because participants in this shadowy game
of "Who am I?"

often come off as
who they're not.

What's seen is not gotten
what's gotten is imagery

of imaginary face.
You must be a medium

rare, but learned of psyche,
to unravel the persona

of unknown dwellers in blackness
toying with chances of fact,

that harm to heal
truth, that lies from ignorance

serenity from searching
the soul.

Classic Rock

ALCOHOL:
Someone else's libations caught my attention,
watched 16 oz. curls on weekdays,
heavyweights workout after Thursday,
Johnnie Walker bench pressed a half-gallon,
Jim Beam a quart,
after sets of 20,
wobbly and weak muscles prevailed,
this liquid gym worked backwards,
nothing being built,
the wrecking ball of life ruled,
monkey do, monkey see
this monkey did and saw
that the monkey was more powerful
than I – that monkey of brass;

CIGARETTES:
Tarzan-like, this monkey's
network of vines let it move from place to place,
fluidly,
it shadowed me through the jungle habitat of life,
on the trail,
when I saw my first camel,
it was there,
he coached my coughing,
taught me how to inhale,
poisons that don't immediately
do harm;

elusiveness – another lesson taught,
see, I had hide and seek techniques,
knowing wrong, I cloaked myself into invisibility
until Mom's x-ray instinct saw through my cover,
whooped my ass, she did,
then comforted me
by letting me eat all the tobacco I wanted.

MARIJUANA:
Speaking of comfort,
on my road to ruin
I met a culprit
that kept me at ease,
Attention Deficit Disorder
as soon as I toked,
lovely I smoked,
split reality in two,
mines and my others

quickly became pals with my monkey,
them two together gave the feeling
of Samson in an era
of non-cutting tools, with hair of steel
that dirty low-down
made my next acquaintance possible.

COCAINE:
crept up on me in it's
shining metallic boat,
powder that I stirred

into my cup of insanity –
increased velocity,
could dance all night –
served as appetizer,
with corruption the entree,
the all you can eat buffet of destruction,
like flour to a cake, my buddy The Chef,
altered the dish by adding water
and a close resemblance to flour itself,
dinner was served.

CLASSIC ROCK:
My voracious appetite for this concoction
stole my hunger for all else,
I was ally and foe,
I fought against white-coated soldiers
whose endless regiment, persistent,
hit one, eye square,
went up in smoke,
cloud so mesmerizing
couldn't wait to waste another, and another, and another,
troops diminished quickly,
had to seek out more,
senses acute,
head swivel left, head swivel right,
as I continuously search for my life's end.

RECOVERY:
Me, whose obsession
was an initiation

into a *la cosa nostra*-like set,
no way out except death,
or telling on myself,
zombie,
connected with legions like me,
"Dawn of the Dead"
now has new meaning,
as wee hours become a buffet line

of half-living creatures
in search of
a meal to stay dead,
picture that, every corner a Kodak moment
and the snapshot stays the same,
only the participants change,
just be careful who you badmouth
I'm no longer saying cheese!

The Choice is Yours

I'm reading this poem I wrote this morning
          on this day of celebration
to try to bring some understanding
          to one serious situation

it's quite confusing to me sometimes
          so I'm going to try and clear the air
don't want to sit for another psycho-social
          let another occupy my chair

some things on this road
          of living life and being free
seem like they contradict themselves
          here's an example for you to see

they told me to be selfish in my recovery
          then they told me I had to give back
they told me I had all the tools I needed
          then they told me what I lacked

they told me to continue to progress
          ride the wave, get in the groove
then told me to sit still and ponder
          before making my next move

I was told to learn, to listen
          so I let others speak the floor
then I was told I was isolated

because I didn't talk no more

on one hand, be honest
        throw up feelings when you get the chance
don't worry if your business is discussed
        at the next recovery dance

then I heard, watch what you say in group
        everything is not for everybody
reveal too much to the wrong individuals
        the police are in the lobby

all in all I've figured it out
        it's the choices that you make
that lead you in the right direction
        the advice that you do take

the changes you decide that make you better
        with some outside intervention
because if it was up to you
        all your faults you would not mention

so to sum this up what I'm trying to say
        is choose wisely in all you do
use consequential thinking like $4 = 2 + 2$
        no matter which way it's said or done

the answer is the same
        if you find out you're not winning
it's time to change your game

just stay centered, think things through

and what you don't like, rearrange
through all the confusion my conclusion is
it's all about what you change!

Line of Sight

The slightest movement of the protector of
the eyes, the window to the soul
the cordless shade whose frilly endings
ward off unwanted visual contortions
shut off the world for a microsecond and
then turns it back on

During that instance world changes have been made
because the tick and tock never stop
even the unseeing have the switch

The manual manipulation of choosing one or the other
flirtatious in nature
the wolves flaunt it
some sheep fall deep

The unthought-of possible nervous condition
a blessing in disguise with any sudden movement
within a perimeter of notice
women bat to perfection
the cougars are good
nubile, keep watch

The cease of action catatonic in nature
can convey one thing in two ways:
the store is no longer open
or is closed for good

JOE ALLEN, JR.

In essence a sign of living
all in the eye, a blink!

Second Chances

In the old testament there was no removal of sin
in the new, you're still running a race you can win

your perspective once being a mistake and you're doomed
but you were being led, being taught, being groomed

I may sound like a soap box preacher , not poet
but you had some chances that you blew and you know it

as we stand and contemplate the time that remains
let's reflect on the chances we can't seem to regain

the loves that you lost when you so desperately tried
you would think that without them you'd surely have died

the time we let lapse between thoughts and progression
the learning not done cause we already mastered the lessons

there were the words spoken that you can't take back
not that you didn't try but that's a skill that we lack

enough about losses there's news to be spread
think about this when you eat, every time you break bread

mistakes are inevitable, no reason to be scared
admit and them keep moving , your life will be spared

as I stand here reciting, I can't be all bad

I'm in the midst of a new chance, I didn't even know I had

I keep thinking failure, but I seem to past all the tests
everyone here has a new chance and definitely are blessed

ever felt like it was over, run over with despair
gave up on the problem like you didn't even care

worried yourself so much that it affected your day
but the problem disappeared, got solved anyway

I'm trying to deliver a message, but I don't know if you hear
the flesh is limited, physical, visible, but the spirit is infinite

I hope I've relayed this in an understanding way
concentrate on other things as you go through your day

if you have faith in whatever you believe
I hope it's like mine cause there's more to achieve

keep your mind in the spirit and watch how it dances
and intelligently embrace all of your second chances.

Fit a New Description

If I wanted to look like you I could
find a clothing shop in the hood
buy a hood
profile like I'm up to no good
purchase me some denim
$225 to get in 'em
jeans that portray
I got swag
material that lets me brag.

Got me some TRUE RELIGION pants
without spiritual chants
no support in the back
saggin', real slack
my congregation is large
no tithing, no charge
with my underwear thin
who'll protect my rear end?

I want to boast about
hereditary genes
the kind
that give me the means
to be responsible
in all I do
take care of me
and a family, too.

34

The policeman
would be my friend
I go out to work
come back in
suspicion level '0'
the real superhero
able to save the day
no matter what comes my way.

I like to be seen
in a different light, I mean
my manly emanation
reveals my denomination
child of the MOST HIGH GOD
recognize the features? Hope it's not
too hard!
See I walk in grace
but I do know my place...

If I wanted to look like you, I could
but I bring something new to the hood
not my name in the paper
for the next income tax caper
I walk with faith and with pride
with my GOD by my side
not to be shot in the street
when my life is incomplete.

I'll make positive gains
While blood still pumps in my veins

PROGRESSION

And when my success story is read
I won't have to be dead,

I'll be alive to show the way!

My Gang

Let me introduce you to my team
we don't carry guns and our teeth don't gleam
no Crip, no Nyeta, no Blood, no King
at least not Latin
our uniform consists of robes of satin.

You think you're tough
come one come all
my crew runs deep
you're guaranteed to fall.

We're suited with armor
helmet, shield, sword, boots
our breastplate deflects
all our enemy shoots
no matter what caliber of ammunition is used
any negativity is spiritually refused.

No wet finger for my tongue
never hunger or thirst
eat and drink plentiful
my preservation is first.

Let me stop bragging
got more work to do
this talking is cheap
let me show you.

PROGRESSION

When it comes down to "who's the baddest"
between your crew and mine
I close my mouth and keep walking
just check out my shine!

<u>In Closing</u>

I really don't feel like sharing today.
Ever experience that?
Can anyone sympathize with me?
The non-communicable state of ego-time,
wanting to be alone,
even in the presence of others.

Delving inward, imploding upon oneself,
the phasing out of company,
in order to be in solitude,
peace within turmoil,
sitting center stage
in a tornado.

Looking out, surveying the havoc wreaked,
this must be the ultimate multitask,
delivering words in this state.
I stand before you
wanting to corner cower
but still be heard,
an oxymoron,
making my presence felt
while slowly disappearing.

Goodnight.

For information regarding featured readings and general author appearances, please visit our website.

www.urbancentigrade.com

www.ingramcontent.com/pod-product-compliance
Lightning Source LLC
Chambersburg PA
CBHW031617040426
42452CB00006B/560